PLANET EARTH

Published in 2018 by Wayland

Written by Michael Bright
Cover illustration by Mark Turner

Editor: Corinne Lucas
Designer: Alyssa Peacock

ISBN: 978 0 7502 9874 2

10 9 8 7 6 5 4 3 2 1

Picture credits: p 4 (t) © De Agostini Picture Library/Contributor/Getty Images; p 4 (b) © NordNordWest/Wikimedia; p 5 (t) © Everett - Art/Shutterstock; p 5 (b) © John Wollwerth/Shutterstock; p 6 © Wikimedia Commons; p 7 (t) © Karen Kaspar/Shutterstock; p 7 (b) © Hung Chung Chih/Shutterstock; p 8 (t) © Holly Kuchera/Shutterstock; p 8 (b) © Lukas Blazek/Dreamstime; p 9 (t) © Hemis/Alamy Stock Photo; p 9 (b) ©UzFoto/Shutterstock; p 10 (t) © Wikimedia Commons; p 10 (b) © Andreas Borchert/Wikimedia; p 11 (t) © Dmitro/ Shutterstock; p 11 (m) © Byelikova Oksana; p 11 (b) © DeAgostini/Getty Images; p 12 © Dorling Kindersley/Getty Images; p 13 (t) © Typ 620.73.451, Houghton Library, Harvard University/Wikimedia; p 13 (b) © Wikimedia Commons; p 14 © Angela Waye/Shutterstock; p 15 (t) © Wikimedia Commons; p 15 (b) © Wikimedia Commons; p 16 © Wikimedia Commons; p 16–17 © Dorling Kindersley/Getty Images; p 17 (tl) © J. Cameron/Wikimedia Commons; p 17 (tr) © London Stereoscopic & Photographic Company/Wikimedia Commons; p 17 (b) © Fotos593/Shutterstock; p 18 © SSPL/Getty Images; p 19 (t) © Wikimedia Commons; p 19 (b) © Everett Historical/Alamy Stock Photo; p 20 © Wikimedia Commons; p 21 (t) © Everett Historical/Shutterstock; p 21 (b) © Wikimedia Commons; p 22 (t) © Stanislaw Tokarski/ Shutterstock; p 22 (b) © milosk50/Shutterstock; p 23 (t) © UniversalImagesGroup / Contributor/Getty images; p 23 (b) © Wikimedia Commons; p 24 (t) © Picsfive/Shutterstock; p 24 (b) © Trinity Mirror/Mirrorpix/Alamy Stock Photo; p 25 (t) © Telia/Shutterstock; p 25 (b) © sjbooks / Alamy Stock Photo; p 26 © Zahir Hossain Chowdhury/Barcro/Barcroft Media/Getty Images; p 27 (t) © Praethip Docekalova/ Shutterstock; p 27 (b) © COP21/Alamy Stock Photo; p 28 (t) © Wikimedia Commons; p 28 (b) © Wikimedia Commons; p 29 (t) © Rich Carey/Shutterstock; p 29 (b) © JBArt/Shutterstock.

Background images and other graphic elements courtesy of Shutterstock.com.

Contents

EARLY MAN

It has taken 4.6 billion years for the Earth to form into the planet it is today, and modern humans have lived on it for just 200,000 years. Modern humans first lived in Africa. Then, between 125,000 and 60,000 years ago, they moved into the ice-free parts of Europe and Asia, and then westwards into North America. They followed the Pacific coast of the Americas southwards, reaching Chile 18,500 years ago.

stone age hunters

The weapons and tools of early man were made from stone, and this is where the Stone Age, which lasted from 3.4 million to a few thousand years ago, gets its name. The early Stone Age people were nomads, meaning they travelled in small groups, made up of several families. They were 'hunter-gatherers' because they hunted large animals and collected plants, but by the late Stone Age they had begun to settle in villages. At first, they had mainly stone, bone and wooden tools, but later they made the bow and arrow, *bolas*, and spear throwers. They learned to fish with *harpoons* and nets made from plant fibres.

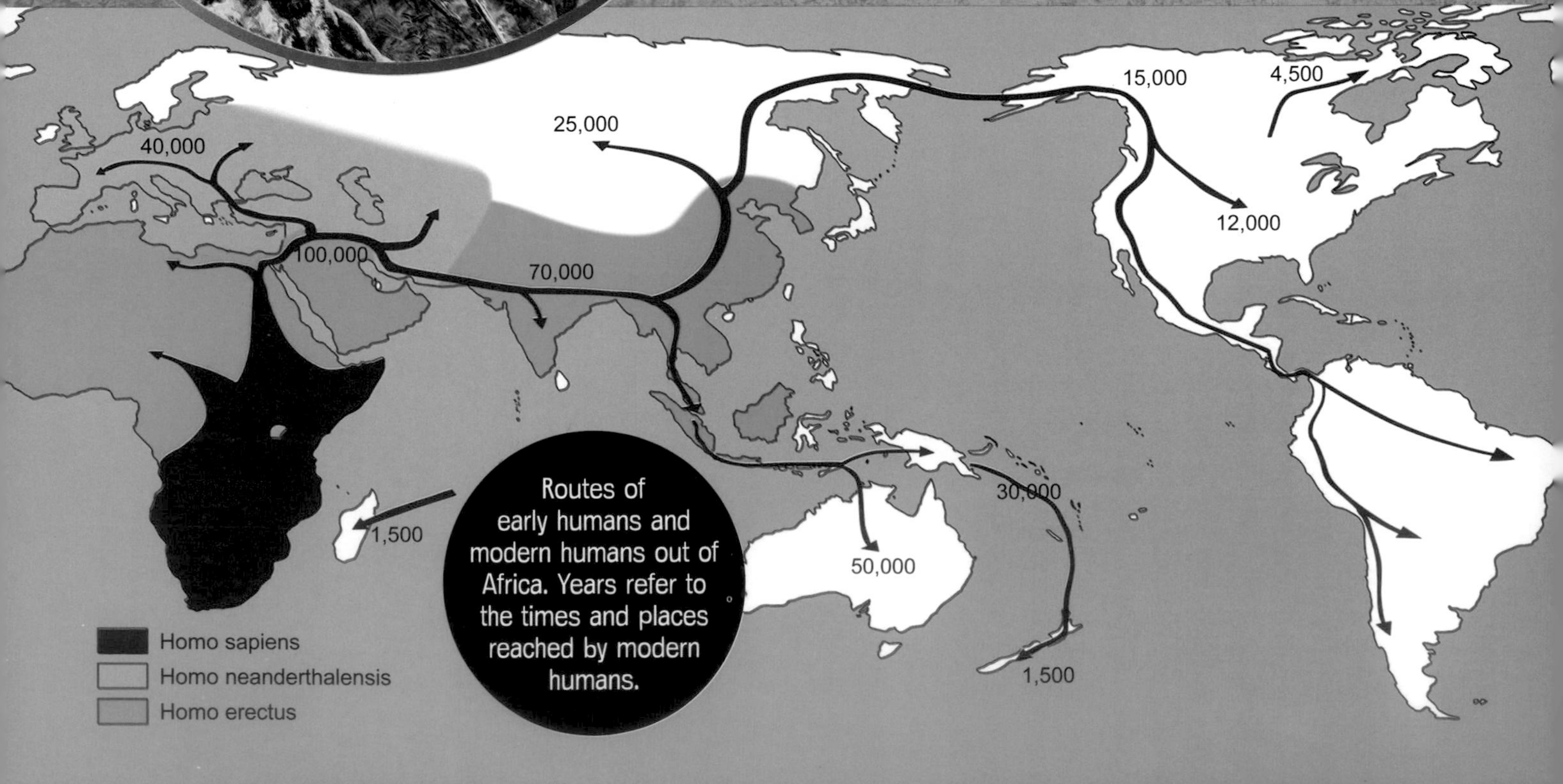

40,000
25,000
100,000
70,000
15,000
4,500
12,000
30,000
50,000
1,500
1,500

Homo sapiens
Homo neanderthalensis
Homo erectus

Routes of early humans and modern humans out of Africa. Years refer to the times and places reached by modern humans.

primitive art

These early people were artists. More than 17,000 years ago, they painted the animals they hunted on cave walls. You can still see examples of this in the caves at Lascaux, southwest France. Artists' paints and materials, such as *ochre*, were probably traded between villages long distances apart, so people had to travel to get them. Art must have been important to them.

telling the time

A *lunar* calendar scratched into a piece of bone has been found in southwest France. It shows the phases of the Moon, and was made about 28,000 years ago. The calendar probably helped hunters to predict when animals on *migration* passed close to their village.

origins of music

The first human music might have been created from everyday activities, such as cracking nuts. The rhythm would have made repetitive chores bearable, in the same way that soldiers used to chant on long marches. Later, humans made flute-like bone pipes and skin drums. The music was possibly performed at religious events.

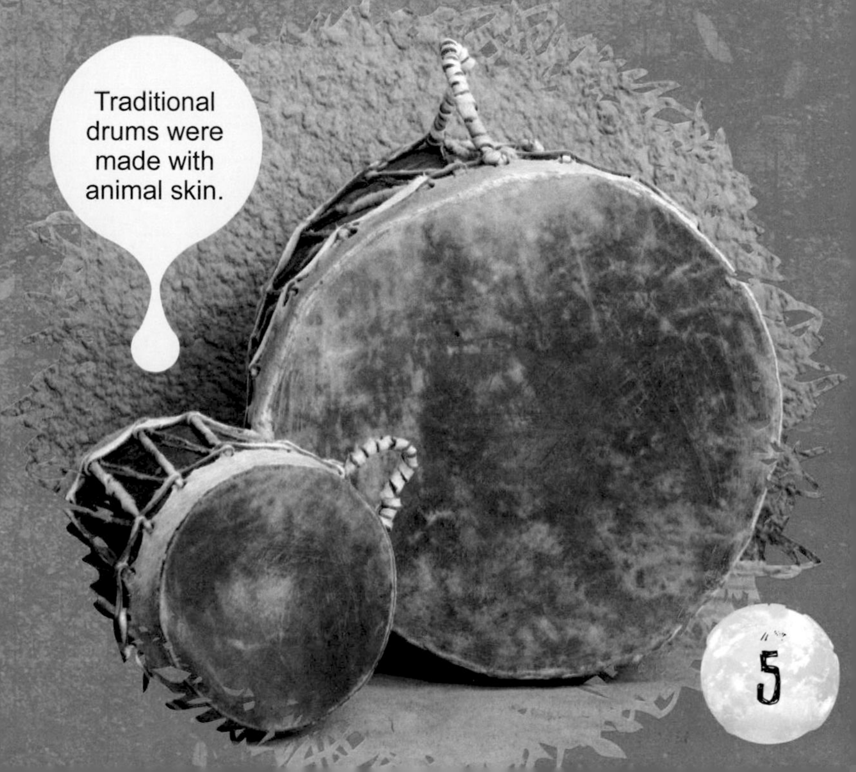

Traditional drums were made with animal skin.

first FARMERS

The last Ice Age drew to a close about 10,200 years ago, and the time period known as the Holocene epoch began. This is the geological time period that we live in today. During this change from one period of time to another, there was also a great change in lifestyle, from people living as hunter-gathers to farming the land instead.

first crops

The change began in the Fertile Crescent in the Middle East, which stretches from ancient Mesopotamia – what is now Iraq, Syria and Kuwait – to the Nile Valley in Egypt. People began to grow and tend to crops: three cereals – emmer and einkorn wheat, and barley; and four legumes – lentil, pea, bitter vetch (similar to lentil) and chickpea.

a world of crops

Agriculture began to develop elsewhere in the world, too. Maize, beans and squash were early crops in the Americas. China gave us rice, millet, soybeans, peaches and oranges. Africa's Ethiopian Highlands were the region where coffee was first harvested, and bananas were first grown in Papua New Guinea.

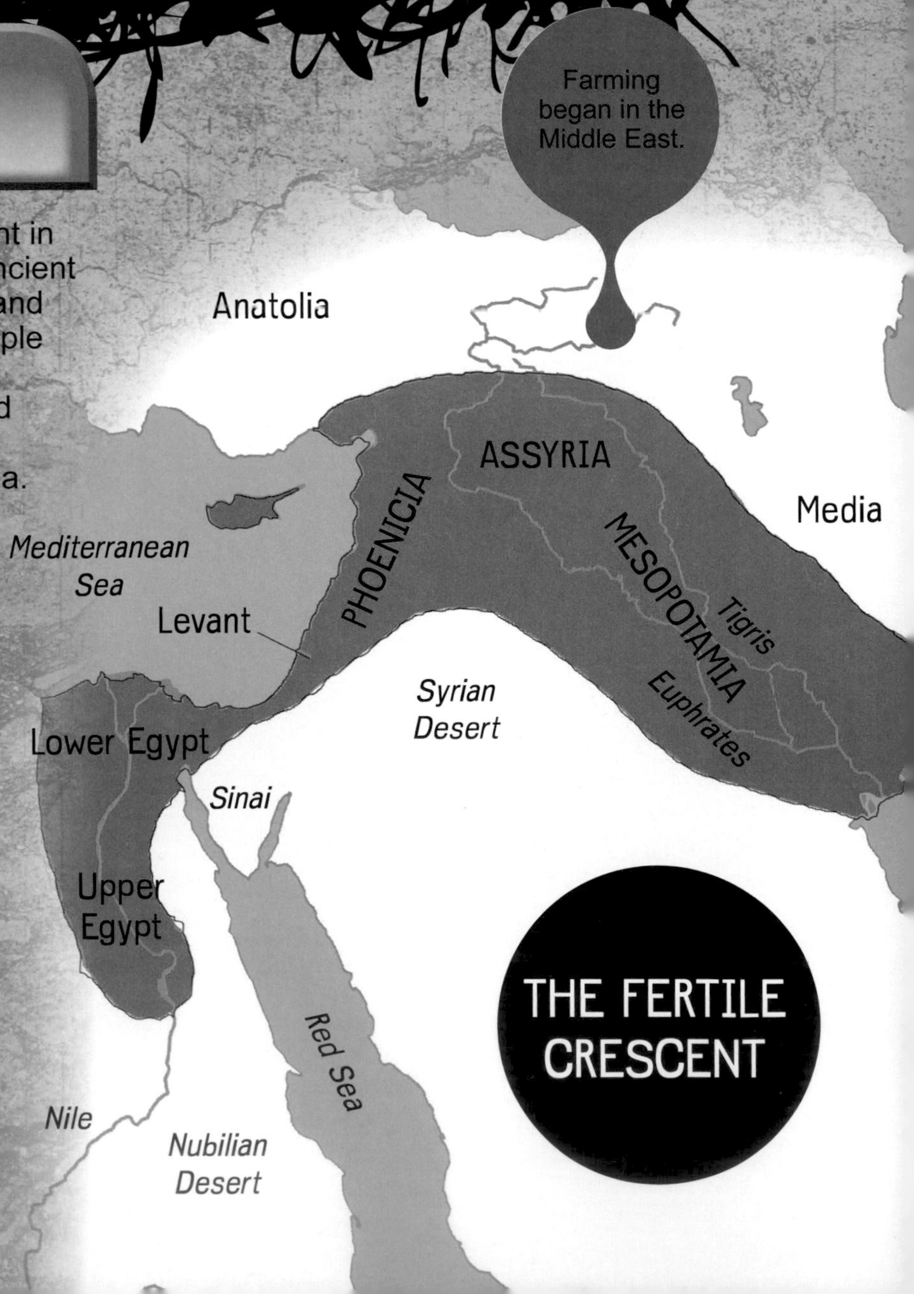

crop rotation

Early Middle Eastern farmers realised they could not grow the same crop every year in the same field or the soil lost its *nutrients*. They did not understand the chemistry, but they knew what worked. They swapped growing wheat, which took up most of the nutrients in the soil, with beans and peas, which added a natural *fertiliser* to the soil.

Emmer wheat was an early crop.

Rice terraces cut into steep slopes.

vital water

With the planting and growing of crops, people needed a way of watering them. It occurred to the early farmers of Mesopotamia that they could grow more crops if they were able to channel water directly from rivers or lakes to their fields. In ancient Egypt, farmers relied on the flooding of their land when the Nile burst its banks each year. Further upstream, the ancient Nubian people used waterwheels to transport the Nile water from the river and onto their land. Early farmers in hill country in China, India and the Americas directed water along *terraces* cut into hillsides.

taming wild ANIMALS

Along with growing wild plants as crops, early farmers also tamed wild animals. They were *tamed* for their meat and milk, and the larger animals were used to carry heavy loads.

wolf in dog's clothing

One of the first animals to be tamed was the wolf. This happened between 30,000 and 15,000 years ago somewhere in *Eurasia*, some time before people started farming. Wolves probably first scavenged meat from humans, and were then encouraged to join the hunt. Eventually, they became dependent on people and the domestic dog was born. The history of every *breed* of dog living today, from the tiny Chihuahua to the biggest Great Dane, can be traced back to an ancient species of wolf.

Dogs evolved from wolves.

farm animals

All our farm animals were once wild creatures. The earliest plant-eater to be farmed was the wild ibex. It was tamed about 11,000 years ago in the Fertile Crescent, where it became the domestic goat. A Eurasian mountain sheep called the mouflon was the source of most of our farmed sheep, and the Eurasian wild boar is the ancestor of the domestic pig. Chickens came from the red jungle fowl of southern Asia.

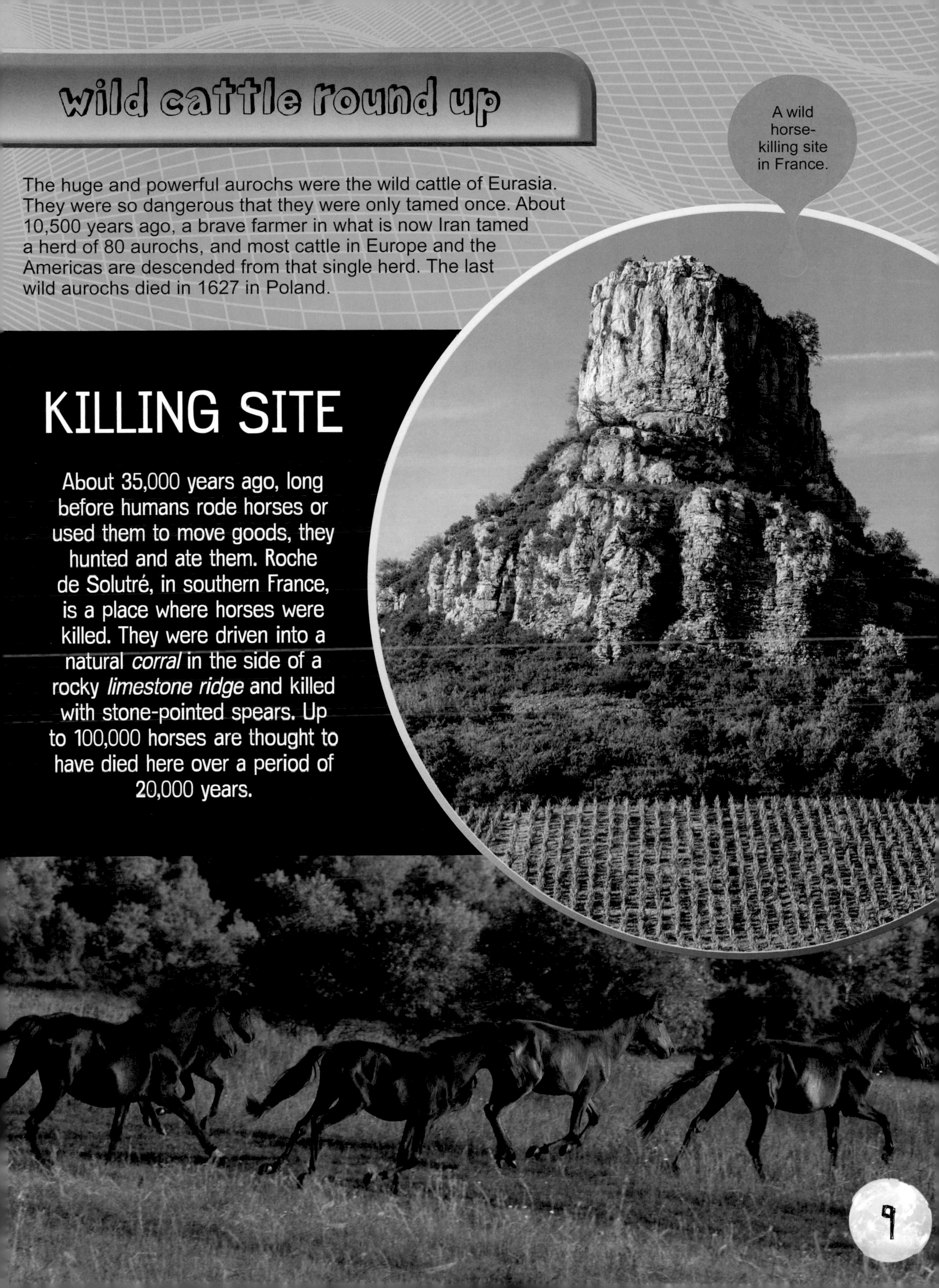

wild cattle round up

The huge and powerful aurochs were the wild cattle of Eurasia. They were so dangerous that they were only tamed once. About 10,500 years ago, a brave farmer in what is now Iran tamed a herd of 80 aurochs, and most cattle in Europe and the Americas are descended from that single herd. The last wild aurochs died in 1627 in Poland.

A wild horse-killing site in France.

KILLING SITE

About 35,000 years ago, long before humans rode horses or used them to move goods, they hunted and ate them. Roche de Solutré, in southern France, is a place where horses were killed. They were driven into a natural *corral* in the side of a rocky *limestone ridge* and killed with stone-pointed spears. Up to 100,000 horses are thought to have died here over a period of 20,000 years.

VILLAGES and TOWNS

Farming brought many changes to people's lives. People stopped travelling, settled in permanent villages, and they each did different jobs. One person grew cereals and another turned them into bread and sold them. Any extra food could be traded with other villages, so some settlements grew to become towns and then great cities.

early money

People traded cattle, sheep and pigs or sacks of grain. Gradually that produce was given a value and money was created. The shekel, for example, was originally worth the same as 180 grains of barley (about 11 g or 0.39 oz). Eventually, when metals were *forged*, coins made of iron, copper, silver and gold became the normal currency. The first known coins are from Anatolia in modern Turkey and the Greek island of Aegina, and are about 2,700 years old. They were made of a natural *alloy* of gold and silver, known as electrum.

Villages became forts to protect people from invaders.

wheels

Trade between people meant that goods had to be transported. At first, farmers carried them on their back. Then, they enlisted the help of cattle and horses, but the great leap forward was the invention of the wheel and a cart that could be pulled by farm animals. Wheels were made of solid wood at first, and appeared about 8,500 years ago.

A Nepalese potter uses a potter's wheel turned by hand.

pottery

The wheel was not used just for transportation. The potter's wheel appeared about the same time as farming. At first, pots were made from long rolls of clay that were coiled around and beaten into the shape of a pot. But by around 6,500 years ago, pots were shaped on a slow-moving potter's wheel.

writing

Middle Eastern traders needed to keep a record of what they bought and sold, so a simple form of writing also developed with farming. There are two examples of the first writing. One was on a piece of wood discovered near Dispilio, Greece, and the other was on clay tablets found in Tartaria, Romania. Both are more than 7,000 years old.

metals and KNOWLEDGE

Metal tools were inventions that marked the Bronze and Iron ages (3300–500 BCE). They were used in farming and as weapons. About the same time, cities of tens of thousands of people, such as Ur and Babylon in Mesopotamia, were founded. They had to be organised by a government who created laws and armies to protect them from unfriendly neighbours. This also meant people began to be divided by their jobs and wealth, and some people even became slaves. It was not unlike the world we live in today.

written word

The Iron Age (1200–500 BCE) gave the world not only iron and steel, but also alphabets and written languages. This was a way of recording history, and the first religious texts appeared at this time, such as the oldest parts of the Hebrew Bible. It also meant people could write down stories that had previously been handed down by word of mouth. It was the birth of literature.

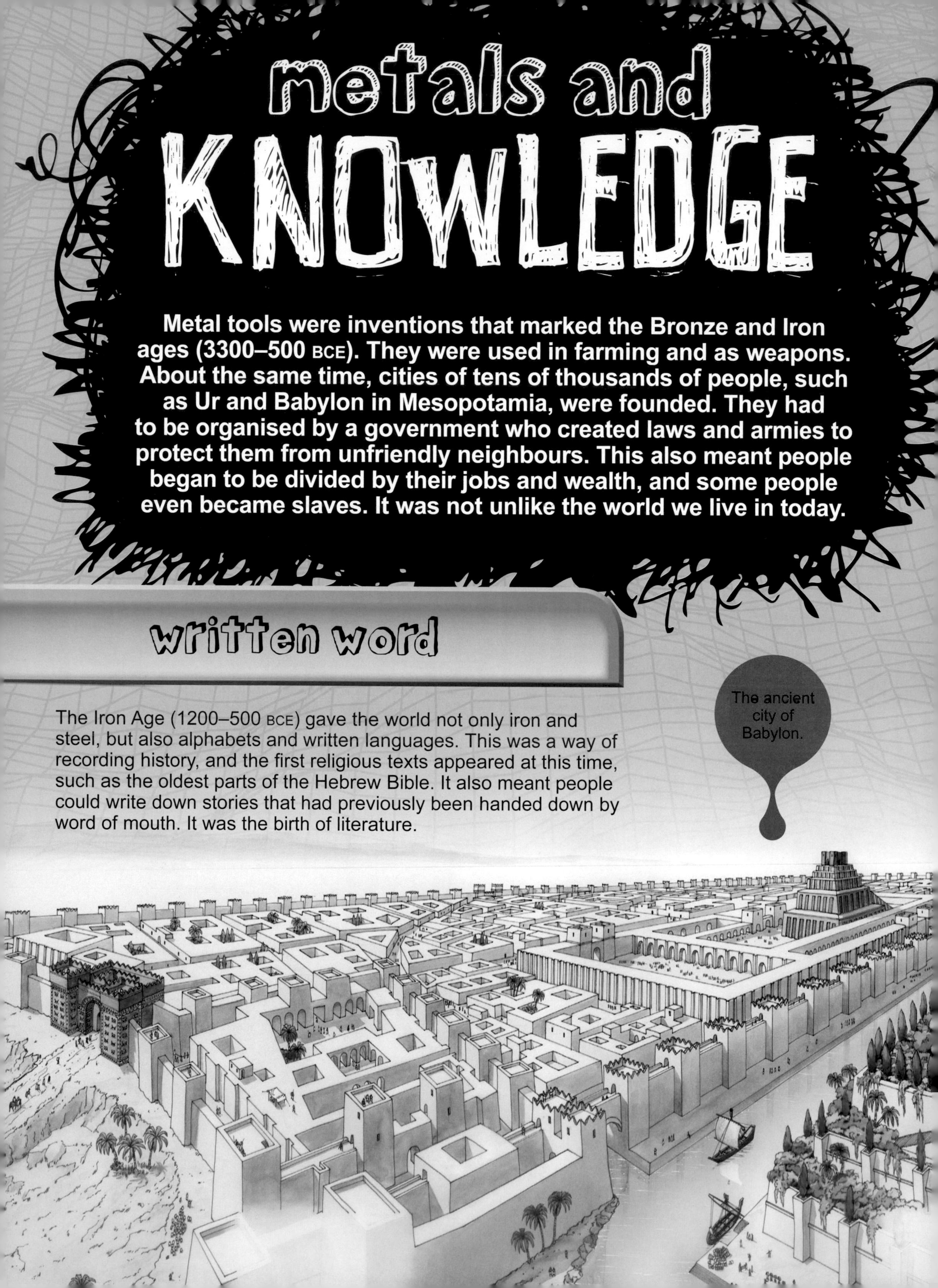

The ancient city of Babylon.

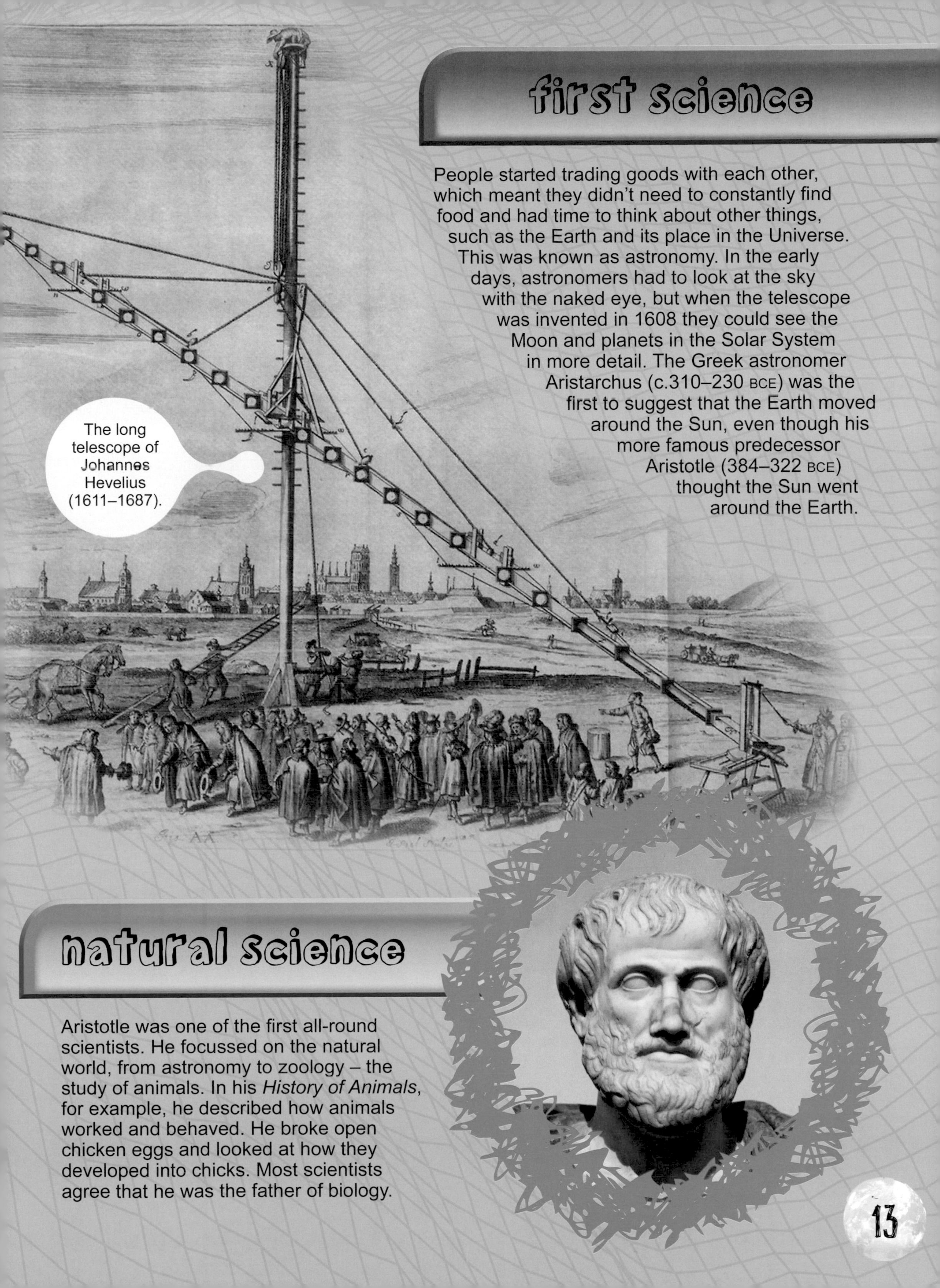

first science

People started trading goods with each other, which meant they didn't need to constantly find food and had time to think about other things, such as the Earth and its place in the Universe. This was known as astronomy. In the early days, astronomers had to look at the sky with the naked eye, but when the telescope was invented in 1608 they could see the Moon and planets in the Solar System in more detail. The Greek astronomer Aristarchus (c.310–230 BCE) was the first to suggest that the Earth moved around the Sun, even though his more famous predecessor Aristotle (384–322 BCE) thought the Sun went around the Earth.

The long telescope of Johannes Hevelius (1611–1687).

natural science

Aristotle was one of the first all-round scientists. He focussed on the natural world, from astronomy to zoology – the study of animals. In his *History of Animals*, for example, he described how animals worked and behaved. He broke open chicken eggs and looked at how they developed into chicks. Most scientists agree that he was the father of biology.

world EXPLORERS

The world's earliest explorers were the people who moved out of Africa and spread across the world. The next explorers were traders from Europe, the Middle East and Asia who set up trading routes across the globe. Amongst them were adventurers who wanted to find out more about the world they lived in.

trading routes

The Spice Route carried spices, such as cinnamon, ginger and pepper, from Asia to the Middle East and Europe by sea. The Silk Road carried goods, such as Chinese silk, from the Far East to the Middle East overland. And the Amber Road transported amber from the Baltic to the Mediterranean and the Middle East. Amber is *fossilised* tree resin, known as the 'gold of the north', and used to make jewellery.

The red line shows the route taken by land and the blue line shows the route taken by sea.

pioneer traders

The Italian trader Marco Polo (1254–1324) was not the first European to reach China, but he was one of the first to write about his experiences. He travelled in Asia for 24 years, bringing back treasures and stories. These inspired another Italian explorer, Christopher Columbus (1450–1506), to search for a route to the Far East by heading west rather than east. Instead, he came across the Americas in 1492, nearly five centuries after the Viking Leif Erikson landed on the coast of what is now Canada.

Et des merveilles

A page from 'The Travels of Marco Polo'.

a round world

Some people used to think that the world was flat, and the explorer who proved that it is round was the Portuguese explorer, Ferdinand Magellan (1480–1521). Like Columbus, he sought a trading route to the Far East by sailing west. He headed for the southern tip of South America, sailing through the *straits* that are now named after him, and into the Pacific Ocean. Magellan was killed before completing the journey, but in 1522 his ships and crews made it all the way around the world.

age of ENLIGHTENMENT

Many scientific explorers of the 18th and 19th centuries were plant and animal collectors. They searched the world for new species, but a few began to use their discoveries to develop ideas about the relationship between life and its surroundings, and how living things change over time.

south american odyssey

The German *naturalist* and explorer Alexander von Humboldt (1769–1859) travelled in South America. He went on foot through jungles, by canoe on the Amazon and Orinoco rivers, and he climbed volcanoes in the Andes. One of his most important discoveries was the link between a region's geography and its plants and animals. He discovered, for example, that plants and animals at the bottom of a mountain were very different from those half way up, and these, were different from those living at the top. He saw this in the Andes mountain chain, but it is the same on mountains all over the world.

a theory of evolution

Charles Darwin

Alfred Russel Wallace

Charles Darwin (1809–1882) and Alfred Russel Wallace (1823–1913) were travellers and collectors who both came up with a *theory* of *evolution* for living things. They realised not every plant or animal in a species is the same, and the ones most suited to where they live are more likely to survive and breed. This is popularly known as the 'survival of the fittest'.

isolated on galápagos

Darwin's ideas came partly from his visit to the Galapagos Islands, off the coast of Ecuador. He found that giant tortoises were different on each island, even though they were probably all descendants of the same species that reached the islands thousands of years before. The tortoises on wet islands, with good plant life, had domed shells and short necks, and ate grasses and vegetation. Those on dry islands had saddleback shells and long necks, and they fed on cacti.

Different species live at different *altitudes* on an Asian mountainside.

The saddle-shelled giant tortoise stretches up to feed on cacti.

age of MACHINES

At about the same time that naturalists were making their discoveries across the world, *engineers* in Britain were starting another revolution. Until the late 18th century, most *manufacturing* was done by hand, but during the 'Industrial Revolution' engineers designed machines that did jobs cheaper and quicker than people.

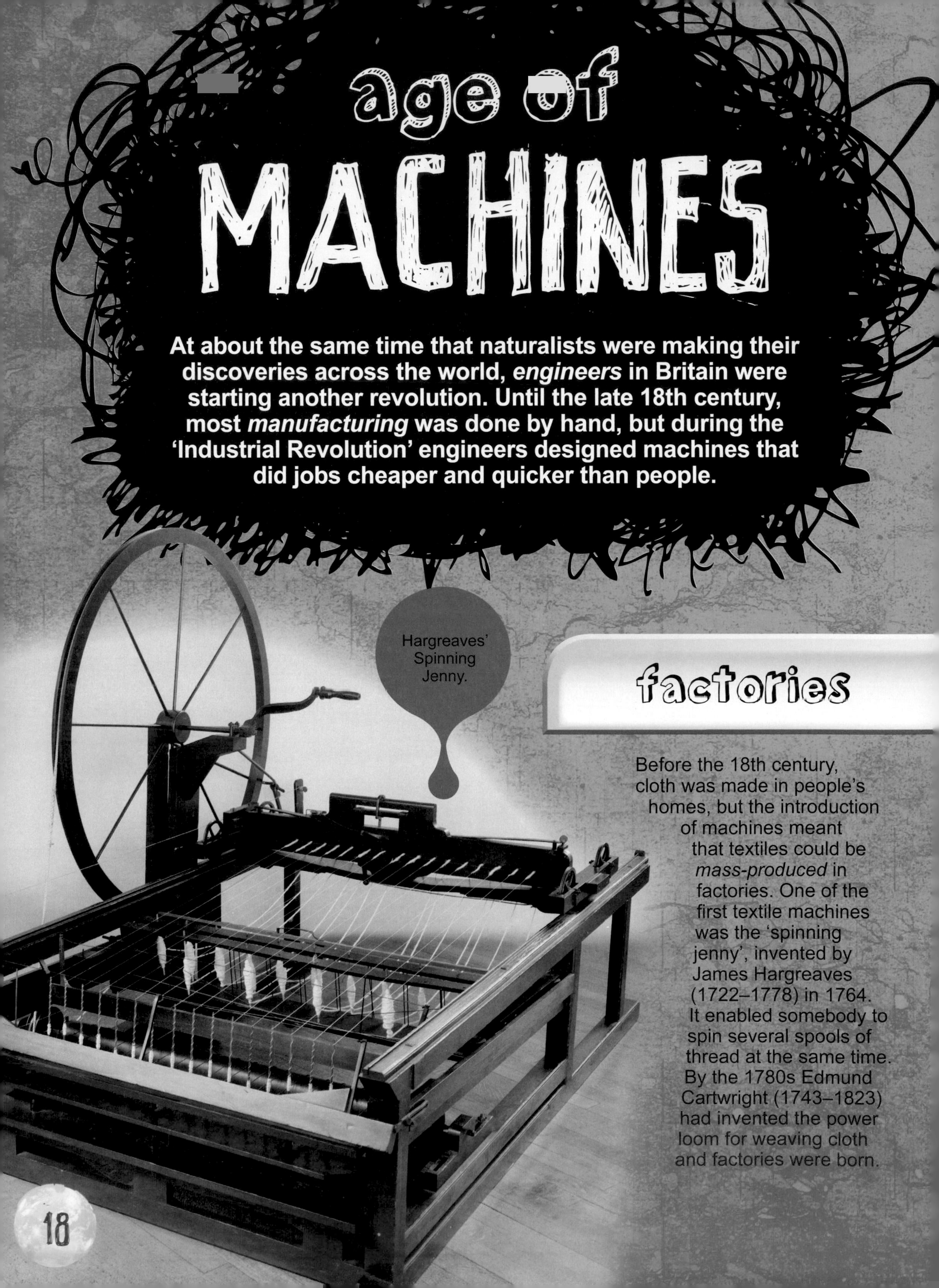

Hargreaves' Spinning Jenny.

factories

Before the 18th century, cloth was made in people's homes, but the introduction of machines meant that textiles could be *mass-produced* in factories. One of the first textile machines was the 'spinning jenny', invented by James Hargreaves (1722–1778) in 1764. It enabled somebody to spin several spools of thread at the same time. By the 1780s Edmund Cartwright (1743–1823) had invented the power loom for weaving cloth and factories were born.

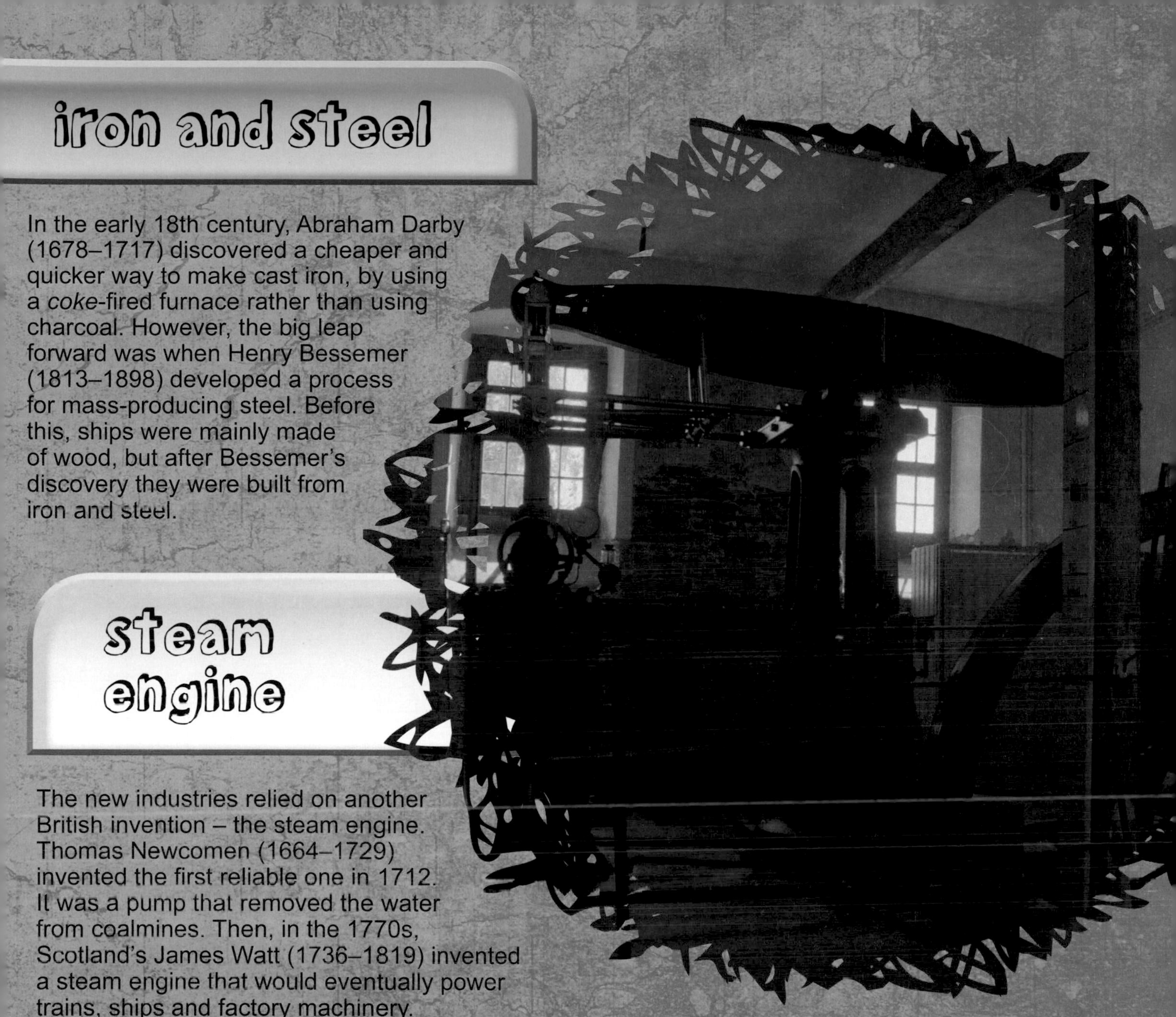

iron and steel

In the early 18th century, Abraham Darby (1678–1717) discovered a cheaper and quicker way to make cast iron, by using a *coke*-fired furnace rather than using charcoal. However, the big leap forward was when Henry Bessemer (1813–1898) developed a process for mass-producing steel. Before this, ships were mainly made of wood, but after Bessemer's discovery they were built from iron and steel.

steam engine

The new industries relied on another British invention – the steam engine. Thomas Newcomen (1664–1729) invented the first reliable one in 1712. It was a pump that removed the water from coalmines. Then, in the 1770s, Scotland's James Watt (1736–1819) invented a steam engine that would eventually power trains, ships and factory machinery.

LUDDITES

Not everyone was a fan of the new machines. Some people tried to destroy factories and the machinery. They were known as 'luddites', a term that is still used today to describe somebody who doesn't like new technology. The name comes from either a weaver named Ned Ludd or another called Ludnam. One of them is supposed to have used a hammer to destroy their knitting machinery.

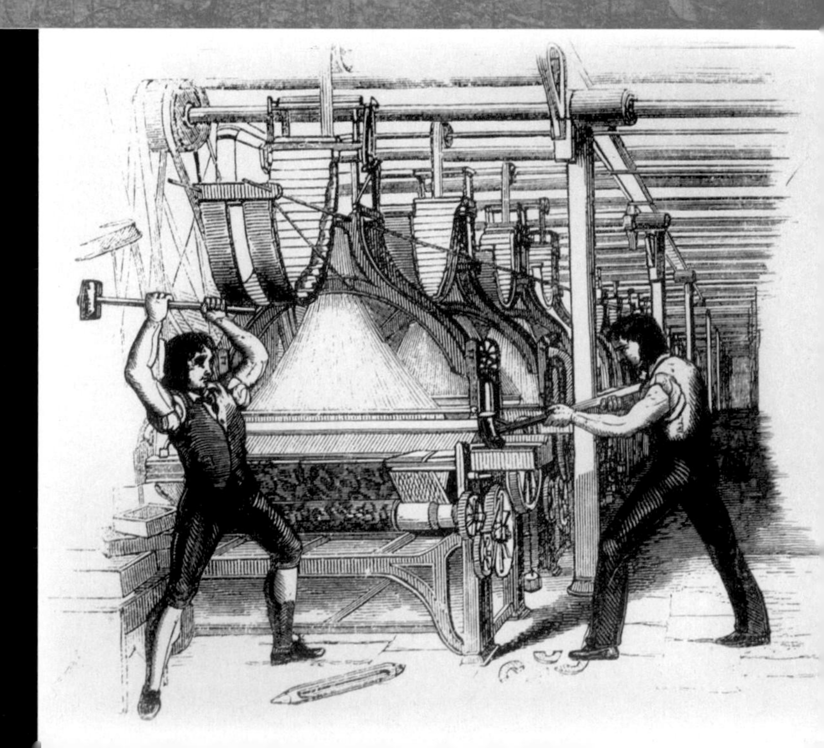

getting ABOUT

Transport changed a lot after the Industrial Revolution. Since the invention of the wheel, goods had been carried on horse-drawn carts (see page 11). Items were also transported in horse-drawn barges along rivers and canals, or moved across the ocean on sailing ships. But all that changed with the invention of engines.

An exact copy of the North River Steamboat.

steamships

There were many experimental steamboats built in the late 18th century, but American engineer Robert Fulton (1767–1815) built the first successful *paddle steamer* – the *North River Steamboat* – in 1807. It sailed along the Hudson River between New York and Albany, in the USA. A little while later, in 1843, British inventor Isambard Kingdom Brunel (1806–1859) designed and built the *S. S. Great Britain*, the forerunner of all modern ships.

flying machines

Ever since watching birds, humans have wanted to fly. In fact, Sir George Cayley (1773–1857), the 'father of the aeroplane', studied birds and how they fly, and developed all sorts of *gliders*. The Wright brothers are credited with the first controlled, powered, heavier-than-air manned flight at Kitty Hawk, North Carolina, USA, on 17 December 1903. The first flight was 37 m (120 ft) and lasted just 12 seconds. Now a double-decker wide-bodied Airbus 380-800 can fly 15,700 km (9,756 miles) from Dallas, USA, to Sydney, Australia, non-stop in a little over 17 hours.

iron horses

The steam locomotive changed travel on land forever. British engineer Richard Trevithick (1771–1833) built the first steam locomotive in 1804. Steam railways led the way until the early 20th century, when diesel and electric locomotives began to take over. Trains are still being reinvented today. Japan's new bullet train is the world's fastest at 603 kpm (374 mph). It doesn't run on rails, but instead it hovers over a special track for an ultra-fast, bump-free ride.

The first flight of the 'Wright Flyer'.

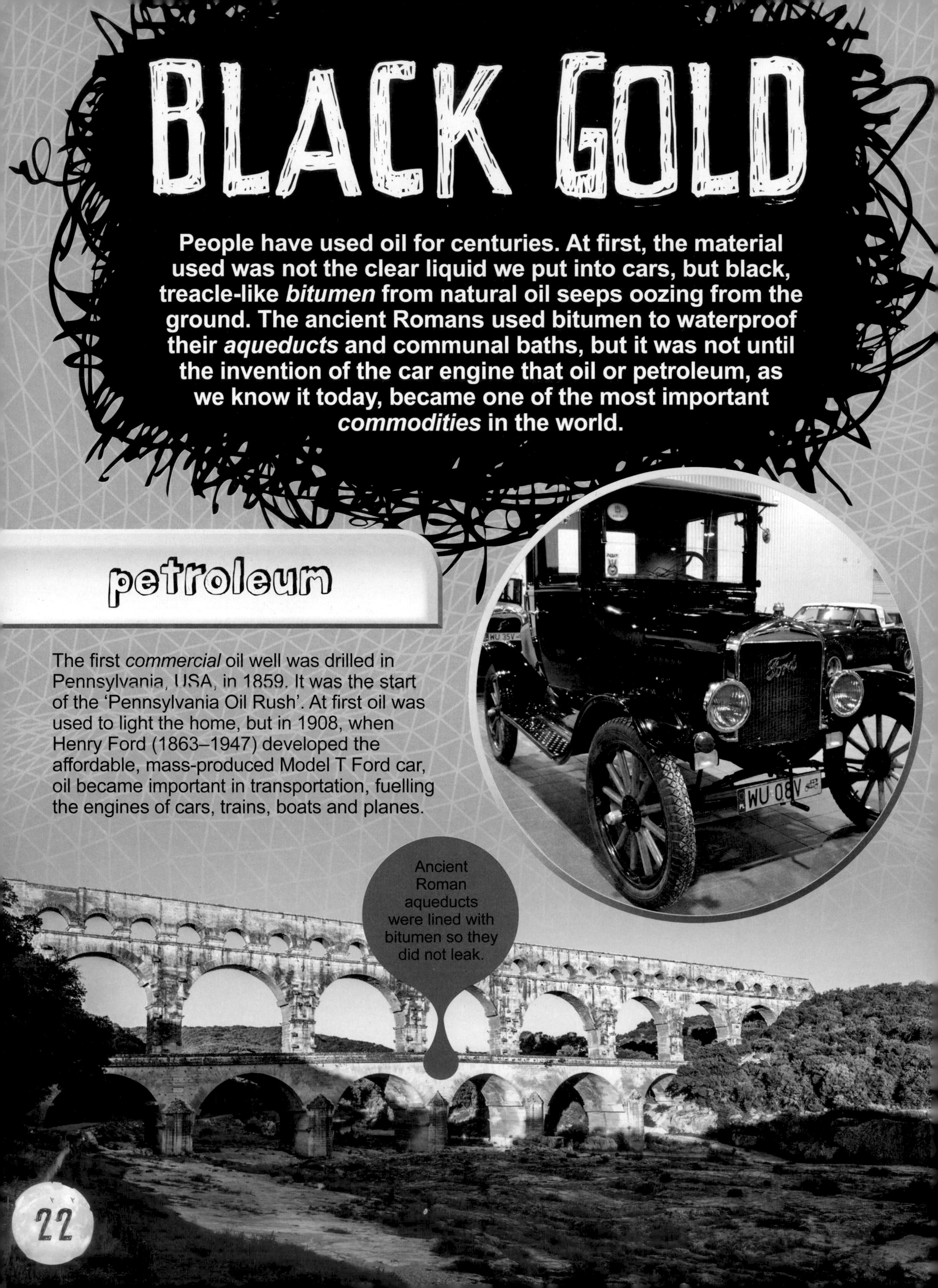

BLACK GOLD

People have used oil for centuries. At first, the material used was not the clear liquid we put into cars, but black, treacle-like *bitumen* from natural oil seeps oozing from the ground. The ancient Romans used bitumen to waterproof their *aqueducts* and communal baths, but it was not until the invention of the car engine that oil or petroleum, as we know it today, became one of the most important *commodities* in the world.

petroleum

The first *commercial* oil well was drilled in Pennsylvania, USA, in 1859. It was the start of the 'Pennsylvania Oil Rush'. At first oil was used to light the home, but in 1908, when Henry Ford (1863–1947) developed the affordable, mass-produced Model T Ford car, oil became important in transportation, fuelling the engines of cars, trains, boats and planes.

Ancient Roman aqueducts were lined with bitumen so they did not leak.

plastics

Oil became more useful than just a fuel. The petrochemical industry make thousands of everyday products, such as plastics, paints, floor wax, detergents, baby oil, toothpaste, tyres, man-made threads and cloths such as nylon, medicines such as aspirin, camping gas, *kerosene* for lamps and heaters, oil to *lubricate* machinery, and asphalt for roads, to name just a few.

Oil derricks that used to drill for oil were first made of wood.

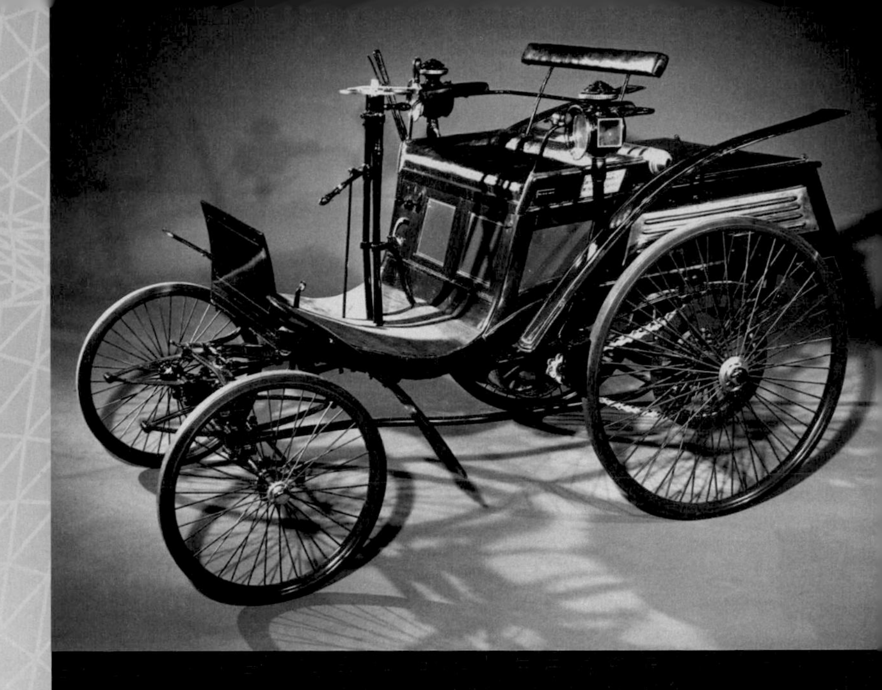

FIRST CARS

Henry Ford did not invent the car, as such. That honour goes to the German engineer Karl Benz (1844–1929). In 1886, he built one of the first cars that drove on public roads. His big break commercially, however, was down to his wife. Bertha Benz took one of the cars and drove her children to her mother's town, the first long-distance journey in a motorcar or 'motorwagen' as it was known. The 1888 event gained the Benz's useful publicity, and it is still celebrated with an antique automobile rally along the 'Bertha Benz Memorial Route' in Germany.

POLLUTION ALERT

The factories of the Industrial Revolution and many of the industries that followed gave us more than just cheap goods – they produced huge amounts of *pollution*. Nobody paid much attention at first, but eventually governments realised that people were dying long before they should.

choking air

One of the first signs of serious pollution was London's Great Smog of 1952. Coal fires in homes, furnaces in factories and the exhausts of cars and lorries created a dense, suffocating fog, called smog. While British 'clean air' laws mean that London is now clear of smog, in other industrial cities, such as Ahwaz in Iran, smog is still a serious health hazard.

hazardous rays

Chemicals known as 'CFCs', which are used in refrigerators and hairsprays, also cause pollution and they destroy the Earth's ozone layer. This is the layer of the *atmosphere* that protects life on Earth from the dangerous rays of the Sun. The pollution has caused an 'ozone hole' over the Southern Hemisphere and many people have suffered from skin cancer because of it.

A London policeman uses a flare to guide traffic in smog.

choked water

Even the open countryside is not safe from pollution problems. Some farmers were pouring huge amounts of fertiliser onto their land. After heavy rains, this was washed into rivers and seas. Here, the fertiliser that helped crops to thrive caused lots of algae to grow in seas and lakes. The algae used up all the oxygen in the water and large areas of the sea, such as the Baltic Sea, became 'dead', with almost no normal marine life.

Thick mats of algae in the Baltic Sea.

A PENGUIN BOOK

Rachel Carson

'... what we have to face is not an occasional dose of poison which has accidentally got into some article of food, but a persistent and continuous poisoning of the whole human environment ...'

Silent Spring

killer chemicals

Another farming problem was the *pesticide* DDT, and several other long-acting pesticides used to kill crop pests. They were found to upset natural systems. In her 1962 book *Silent Spring*, Rachel Carson (1907–1964) highlighted the danger to birds. DDT caused their eggshells to thin and their offspring to die. Carson was one of the first scientists to raise the question of humankind's impact on nature.

WINDS of CHANGE

One of the greatest dangers to the wellbeing of life on Earth is something we take very much for granted – heating and lighting homes. The generation of electricity has a harmful side effect: it could change the *climate* of the Earth. However, there are signs people are going to try and change that.

fossil fuels

For decades, oil, coal and natural gas have been the key sources of energy for transport, for heating and lighting homes and factories, and for the generation of electricity. They are known as 'fossil fuels', because they are the chemicals left behind by the bodies of plants and animals that died millions of years ago breakdown. The problem is that when burned, they release carbon dioxide, a 'greenhouse gas'. Greenhouse gases trap the warmth from the Sun in the atmosphere, in the same way that glass traps heat in a gardener's greenhouse.

Low countries, like Bangladesh, already suffer flooding from the sea.

global warming and climate change

One of the effects of producing greenhouse gases is that the air temperature on Earth rises. Just a few degrees can have a huge impact, causing changes of climate all over the world. Hot, dry regions become even hotter and drier, and normally cooler regions experience extremes of weather. Even scarier is that the Arctic and Antarctic ice sheets could melt, causing the sea level to rise and drown coastal areas and islands.

renewables and non-renewables

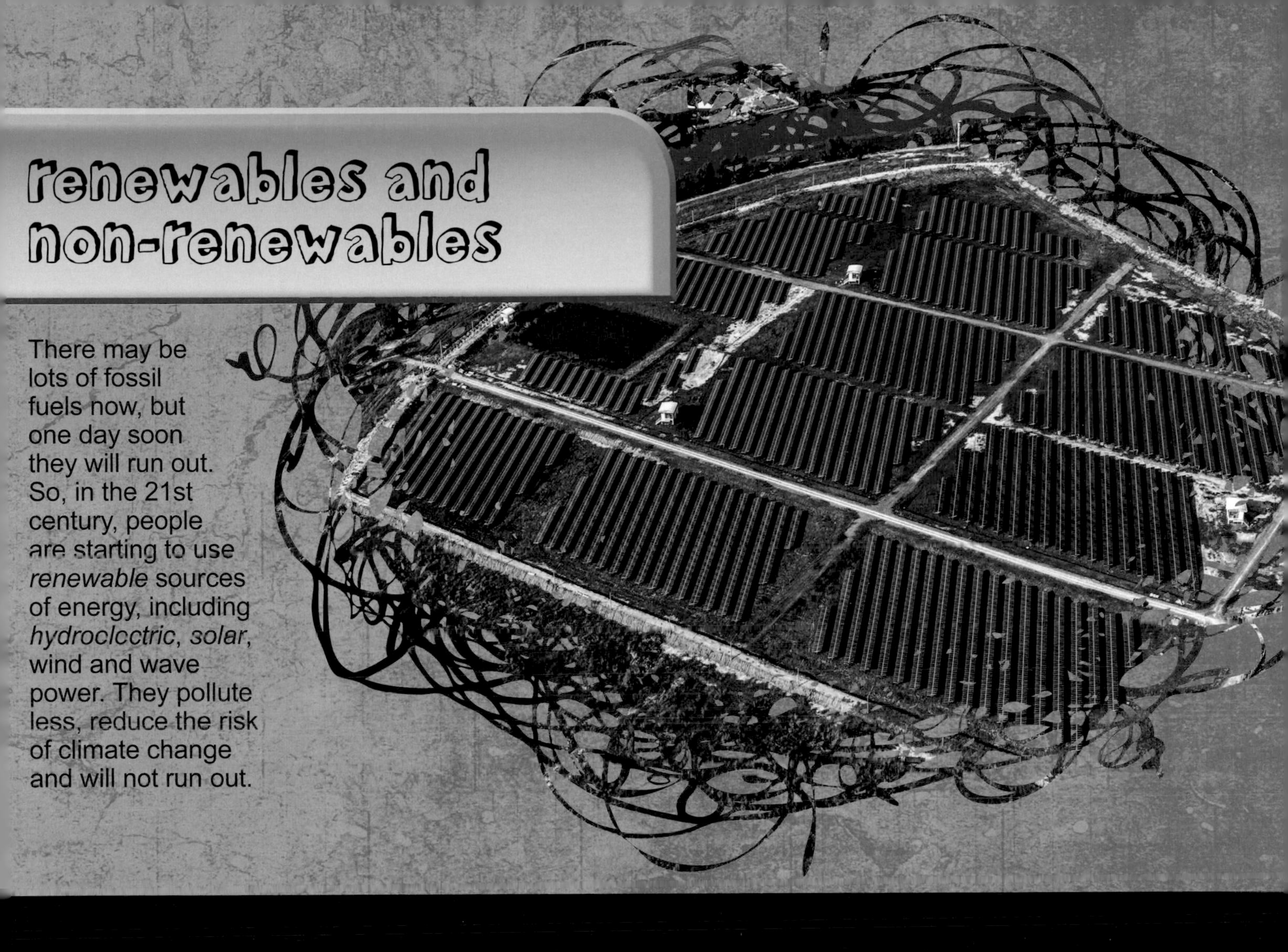

There may be lots of fossil fuels now, but one day soon they will run out. So, in the 21st century, people are starting to use *renewable* sources of energy, including *hydroclcctric*, *solar*, wind and wave power. They pollute less, reduce the risk of climate change and will not run out.

BACK FROM THE BRINK

The world is now acting to help stop climate change. In 2015, at a United Nations Conference in Paris on Climate Change, 196 nations reached an agreement to limit global warming to 2°C (3.6°F), and to reduce the amount of greenhouse gases from human activities to zero during the second half of the 21st century.

a future for PLANET EARTH?

In the USA alone, one person is born every 8 seconds, one person dies every 11 seconds, and the population grows every 16 seconds. The pattern is repeated all over the world, and it adds up to a global population of more than 7.2 billion people. It means humans compete for food and space with all the other living things on our planet, and the non-humans are losing out.

sixth major extinction

There have been five major *mass extinction* events in the history of the Earth. Now, scientists believe there is a sixth, and humans are the cause. Since 1500 CE, nearly 900 species of large plants or animals, such as the dodo and the quagga, are known to have become extinct, but the disappearance of most goes unnoticed. 'It is estimated that dozens of species of plants, animals and microbes become extinct everyday, so up to 50 per cent could disappear by mid-21st century.'

too little, too late?

In 1992, 196 countries signed up to the Convention on Biological Diversity in Rio de Janeiro. It is one of many international agreements aimed at saving the huge range of species on Earth and the places in which they live. Whether these agreements will have any impact and reverse current trends is still to be seen.

on the brink

Even though people are trying to help, humans are still the reason that lots of areas of land have been destroyed, and animals can't survive in oceans, which is killing off thousands of species. It is very clear that humans have had the biggest influence on the planet of any known animal, and in a very short space of time. If we mess things up completely, the human race could migrate again, just as our African ancestors did tens of thousands of years ago. But this time we would be heading to outer space to settle on another planet.

glossary

alloy	a mixture of two or more metals, or metals and non-metals
altitude	height of an object above sea level or ground level.
aqueduct	a bridge carrying a channel of flowing water
atmosphere	layers of gases around a planet
bolas	a rope with weights attached to tie up the legs of a hunted animal
climate	the weather conditions that exist in a particular part of the world
coke	a fuel made from coal
commercial	buying or selling things
corral	an enclosure for confining livestock
detergent	a substance without soap used for cleaning
engineer	a person trained in the design, manufacture and operation of useful machines and structures
Eurasia	the continents Europe and Asia
evolution	a gradual process by which something changes into a better form
fertiliser	a chemical used to make soil better for growing crops
forge	to shape by heating and hammering
fossilised	where once living tissues are replaced by minerals
glider	an aircraft without an engine that moves on air currents
harpoon	a spear attached to a rope that is thrown to kill animals
hydroelectric	electricity generated by the movement of water
kerosene	a fuel made from petroleum, used to power aircraft or in 'paraffin' heaters
limestone	a form of rock made from skeletons of ancient sea creatures
lubricate	to put oil or other substances on to the moving parts of a machine so it runs better
lunar	to do with the Moon
manufacturing	the making of goods
mass extinction	the disappearance of many plants and animals at the same time
mass-produced	making of good in very large quantities
migration	the movement of humans or animals from one place to another
naturalist	a person who studies nature, including wild plants and animals
nutrient	the goodness in food or soil
ochre	an earthy colour varying from yellow to brown and red
paddle steamer	a boat with a steam engine that is moved by large paddles rather than a propeller
pesticide	a chemical used to kill pests, such as crop pests
pollution	a waste product that makes water or air harmful
renewable	not in short supply when used
ridge	a long, narrow raised piece of land
solar	to do with the Sun
strait	a narrow channel joining two large bodies of water
terrace	a horizontal strip of ground that is often one of several on the side of a hill
theory	an idea that is not proven but generally accepted by scientists as true

index

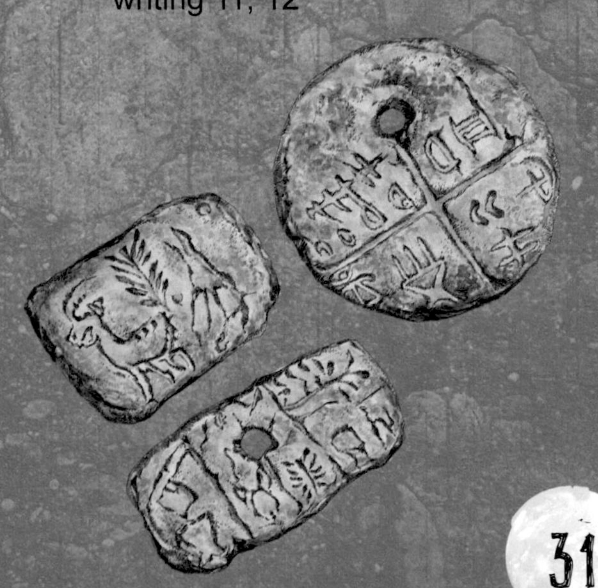

further information

Books

Archaeology: an introduction (2010)
Kevin Green and Tom Moore
Routledge
ISBN-13: 978-0415496391

Horrible Histories (10 Book Set)
Scholastic
ISBN-13: 978-9999252805

Life During the Industrial Revolution (2015)
Anita Ganeri
Raintree
ISBN-13: 978-1406270617

The Industrial Revolution for Kids (2014)
Cheryl Mullenbach
Chicago Review Press
ISBN-13: 978-1613746905

Projects for a Healthy Planet: Simple Environmental Experiments for Kids (1992)
Shar Levine
Jossey-Bass
ISBN-13: 978-0471554844

Planet Earth: 25 Environmental Projects You Can Build Yourself (2007)
Kathleen M. Reilly and Farah Rizvi
Nomad Press
ISBN-13: 978-1934670040

DVDS

Human Planet (2011)
BBC
ASIN: B004EPYSB4

Horrible Histories: Series 1–6
2entertain
ASIN: B011BYQ1VA

Websites

Young Archaeologists' Club
http://www.yac-uk.org

Young People's Trust for the Environment
http://ypte.org.uk

Air Pollution Detectives
http://children.scottishairquality.co.uk

National Geographic Kids
http://ngkids.co.uk

Durrell Wildlife Conservation Trust
http://www.durrell.org/kids